Barbed wire. Majdanek KZ; near Lublin, Poland

Barbed wire. Natzweiler KZ; near Le Struthof, France

AUSCHWITZ BELZEC BERGEN-
BELSEN BIRKENAU BUCHENWALD
BULLENHUSER DAMM CHELMNO

IN THE CAMPS

ERICH HARTMANN

DACHAU EMSLAND FOREST OF
BELOW GROSS ROSEN MAJDANEK
MAUTHAUSEN NATZWEILER NEUEN-
GAMME RAVENSBRÜCK SACHSEN-
HAUSEN SOBIBOR THERESIENSTADT
TREBLINKA VUGHT WESTERBORK

W. W. Norton & Company / New York · London

Text and photographs © 1995 Erich Hartmann
Journal entry in Afterword © 1995 Ruth Bains Hartmann
Quotes on page 11 by Arthur Miller from *New York Times Magazine* © 1963
and *Timebends* © 1987; used by permission of the author

Library of Congress Cataloging-in-Publication Data
Hartmann, Erich, 1922–
    In the camps / Erich Hartmann.
        p.   cm.
1. World War. 1939–1945—Concentration camps—Europe—Pictorial
works.   2. World War. 1939–1945—Prisoners and prisons, German—
Pictorial works.   3. Holocaust, Jewish (1939–1945)—Pictorial works.
I. Title.
D805.A2H35   1995
940.54'72—dc20   94-42756

ISBN 0-393-03772-X

W.W. Norton & Company, Inc., 500 Fifth Avenue, New York, N.Y. 10110
W.W. Norton & Company Ltd., 10 Coptic Street, London, WC1A 1PU

1 2 3 4 5 6 7 8 9 0

"KZ" is the abbreviation of the German term "Konzentrationslager"
(concentration camp) and was used *informally* throughout the system
during the nearly thirteen years of the operation of the camps.
The official designation was "KL," derived from the same term, used
by the camp authorities in correspondence and other documents.

Barbed wire. Birkenau KZ;   Barbed wire. Buchenwald KZ;
Oswiecim, Poland (front endpapers)   near Weimar, Germany (facing page)

Barbed wire. Birkenau ᴋᴢ; Oswiecim, Poland

Dedicated to the memory of the men,
women, and children who were destroyed
in the concentration camps
                and to my wife,
                our children,
                and their children.

Barbed wire. Auschwitz KZ;
Oswiecim, Poland

What is the lesson? It is immensely difficult to be human precisely because we cannot detect our own hostility in our own actions. It is tragic, fatal blindness, so old in us, so ingrained that it underlies the first story in the Bible.

Arthur Miller,
"Our Guilt for the World's Evil,"
New York Times Magazine, 1963

But the truth, the first truth, probably, is that we are all connected, watching one another. Even the trees.

Arthur Miller,
Timebends, 1987

Railroad ramp. Buchenwald KZ; near Weimar, Germany

Remains of rail line toward Poland. Theresienstadt Ghetto; Terezin, Czech Republic

Entrance gate to prisoner cells. Theresienstadt Gestapo prison; Terezin, Czech Republic
Imprisoned here were political opponents of many nationalities as well as some Jews from the nearby Ghetto. The words over the arch announce that WORK MAKES YOU FREE.

Sobibor railroad station; Sobibor, Poland
A branch line led from this station into the woods to the death camp of Sobibor where prisoners were gassed on arrival.

Perimeter wall (1961). Mauthausen KZ; Mauthausen, Austria

Guard towers and memorial of ashes. Majdanek KZ; near Lublin, Poland

Treblinka railroad station; Treblinka, Poland
     A rail spur led directly into the death camp where in fourteen months
of operation 750,000 to 870,000 Jews were gassed. After September 1942
the railroad station was closed to normal passenger traffic in order to expedite
the deportation transports and the killing process.

Railroad tracks toward Auschwitz KZ. Oswiecim railroad station; Oswiecim, Poland

Himmler: "The existing extermination centers in the East are not sufficient to cope with an operation on such a scale. . . . I have designated Auschwitz . . . both because of its convenient location as regards communication and because the area can be easily isolated and camouflaged."

Camp main street. Birkenau KZ; Oswiecim, Poland
    Built on swampy ground, many of the 300 buildings had no flooring.
Over 60 structures still stand in this the largest of the death camps,
3 kilometers from Auschwitz. Precise numbers of dead are unknown because
most arrivals were gassed at once without registration or identification.

Main entrance. Birkenau KZ; Oswiecim, Poland

    A few yards beyond the gate was the end of the line, near the gas chambers. Although the rail system had to meet the needs of war on two fronts, no scheduled transport failed to move.

Selection ramp. Birkenau KZ; Oswiecim, Poland

    Deportees were unloaded from the freight cars here and inspected by SS camp personnel, including doctors. Those found fit for work were separated. The majority, including the old, the sick, most women and children, were sent directly to the gas chambers.

View from the main tower.
Birkenau KZ; Oswiecim, Poland
    *Largest of the extermination
camps, Birkenau covered an area
of over 425 acres. Of more than 300
original buildings, 45 of brick and
22 of wood are still standing.*

Main gate. Buchenwald KZ; near Weimar, Germany

The slogan reads TO EACH HIS OWN. *No one knows the origin of or the reason for maxims such as this throughout the camp system.*

Main gate. Dachau KZ; Dachau, Germany
   Dachau, first of the concentration camps, was set up on March 22, 1933,
near Munich. ARBEIT MACHT FREI (WORK MAKES YOU FREE) *appeared*
at the entrance to many of the concentration camps.

Shoes in showcase. Auschwitz ᴋᴢ; Oswiecim, Poland
A top-secret document of February 6, 1943, from the Reich Ministry
of Economics listed among almost three million kilograms of clothing
from Auschwitz and Majdanek 31,000 men's, 11,000 women's, and 22,000
children's shoes to be redistributed to "ethnic Germans."

Suitcases in showcase. Auschwitz KZ; Oswiecim, Poland

 *Jews to be deported were instructed to take a knapsack or suitcase with
specific belongings including a coat, two pairs of shoes, three sets of underwear,
two suits (men), two summer and two winter dresses (women), warm gloves,
caps, sweaters, etc.* "EVERYTHING MUST BE IN GOOD CONDITION!"

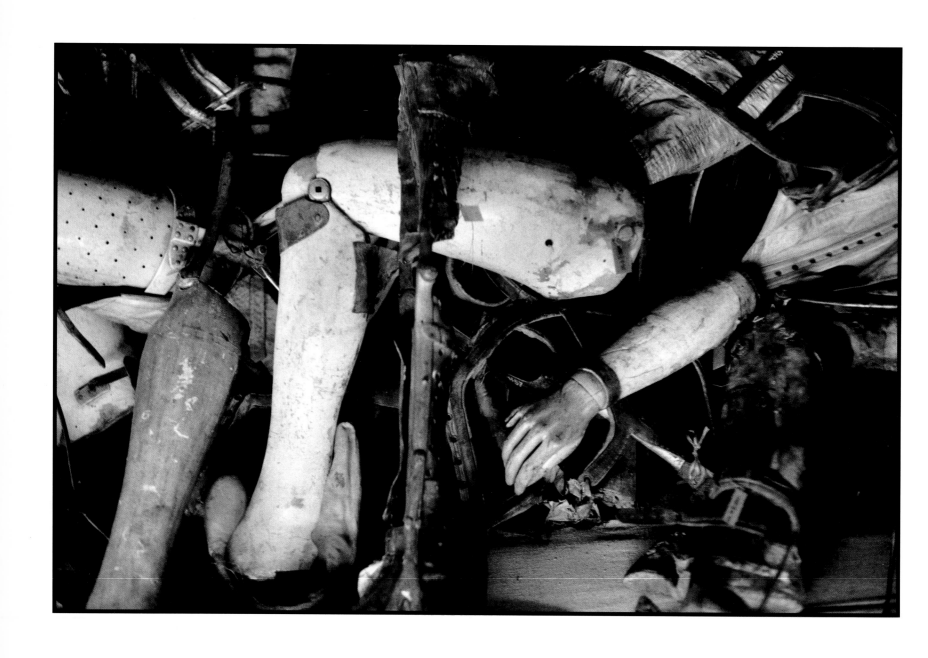

Artificial limbs in showcase. Auschwitz KZ; Oswiecim, Poland
*Everything was confiscated on arrival, sorted, stored, and sent back
to Germany as freight car space was available and timetables allowed.*

Children's clothes in showcase. Auschwitz KZ; Oswiecim, Poland
 More than a million children and infants are known to have perished in the Nazi camps.

Prisoner's uniform. Forest of Below; near Wittstock, Germany

Worn and donated by a Dutch survivor of Sachsenhausen KZ. On arrival at a camp, those who were not immediately killed had their heads shaved, were given a number, a striped uniform, and a pair of sandals or clogs. These garments were not replaced and so had to be constantly repaired.

Kitchen and laundry building.
Dachau KZ; Dachau, Germany
    Painted on the roof was the following slogan: THERE IS ONE ROAD TO FREEDOM. ITS MILESTONES ARE CALLED OBEDIENCE, INDUSTRIOUSNESS, HONESTY, ORDER-LINESS, CLEANLINESS, SOBRIETY, TRUTH-FULNESS, A WILLINGNESS FOR SACRIFICE AND LOVE OF THE FATHERLAND.

Slogans on barracks rafters. Birkenau KZ; Oswiecim, Poland
The slogans read "Cleanliness means Health"; "Be honest";
"Keep Order"; "Honesty lasts the longest."

Wooden barracks. Birkenau KZ; Oswiecim, Poland
Originally Polish cavalry stables intended for 52 horses, each building
later held as many as 1,000 prisoners in three-tiered bunks.

Dayroom. Theresienstadt Gestapo prison; Terezin, Czech Republic

Dayroom. Gross Rosen KZ; Rogoznica, Poland

     Long hours of forced labor in the adjacent stone quarry and little food or
rest accounted for many deaths at Gross Rosen. The estimated number
of prisoners was 125,000, consisting of Jews, Poles, political prisoners of many
nationalities, and Soviet prisoners of war.

Pallet. Buchenwald KZ; near Weimar, Germany

Windowless barracks held as many as 1,500 prisoners in four-tiered wooden bunks. They slept four to a pallet on rotting straw, covered—if at all— with thin blankets or rags.

Toilet in barracks. Theresienstadt Gestapo prison;
Terezin, Czech Republic

Boots of "Moors Soldiers" in museum. Emsland Document Center;
Papenburg, Germany
 *In August 1933, fifteen work camps were established near the Dutch
border where 10,000 political prisoners were used as a slave labor force
to drain the moors. They are memorialized as "The Peat Bog Soldiers" in a
prisoners' song of the time.*

Brick factory and wagon. Neuengamme KZ; Hamburg, Germany
Slave labor built the factory and made bricks here for the SS-owned firm German Earth and Stoneworks.

Quarry cart with rocks. Buchenwald κz; near Weimar, Germany
*Punishment labor at Buchenwald consisted of quarrying stone, which the
SS sold at a profit. Life expectancy at hard-labor camps was a few months.*

Execution slope in stone quarry. Buchenwald KZ;
near Weimar, Germany
  *Prisoners too exhausted to continue to work in the quarry
were summarily shot at this slope.*

"Staircase of Death." Mauthausen KZ; Mauthausen, Austria

Prisoners were forced to carry on their shoulders huge blocks of stone from the quarry below up 186 steps. Many fell or were pushed to their death on the rocks below. The original rough-hewn, uneven steps have been repaired for visitors' safety.

Infirmary. Theresienstadt Gestapo prison; Terezin, Czech Republic
*A few of the original beds. This room would have been crowded with as
many beds as would fit, fastened together in tiers.*

Dissection tables in medical barracks. Sachsenhausen KZ;
Sachsenhausen, Germany
  *Prisoners were routinely used for medical experiments such as new
inoculations, poison gassing, sterilization, reactions to high-altitude conditions,
tolerance to heat and cold, sometimes without an anesthetic. After death,
some organs and tissues were removed for laboratory examination.*

Dissection table. Vught KZ; s'Hertogenbosch, Netherlands

Autopsy table in medical barracks. Natzweiler KZ; near Le Struthof, France

Dissection table. Mauthausen KZ;
Mauthausen, Austria

Gate to cells for political prisoners.
Mauthausen KZ; Mauthausen, Austria

Penal barracks.
Dachau KZ; Dachau, Germany

Isolation cells for political prisoners. Theresienstadt
Gestapo prison; Terezin, Czech Republic

Isolation cell in political block. Mauthausen KZ;
Mauthausen, Austria

Gestapo courtroom in death bunker.
Auschwitz KZ; Oswiecim, Poland
Being sentenced here meant either summary execution at the wall outside or being put into one of the punishment cells in the basement.

Flogging bench. Natzweiler KZ;
near Le Struthof, France (page 62)

Punishment cell in death bunker.
Auschwitz KZ; Oswiecim, Poland
(page 63)

Roll-call square with gallows.
Natzweiler KZ; near Le Struthof, France
 *Hangings took place in front of the
assembled prisoners and were carried out so
as to ensure a slow death.*

Gas chamber. Majdanek KZ; near Lublin, Poland
 At Majdanek 500,000 prisoners were gassed, drowned, shot, hanged,
or given lethal injections.

Gas chamber (reconstruction). Mauthausen KZ; Mauthausen, Austria
Camouflaged as a bathroom with dummy shower heads and drains,
it was partially destroyed by the SS in April 1945.

Gas chamber. Auschwitz KZ; Oswiecim, Poland

    Most Jews deported to Auschwitz were gassed on arrival without identification or registration. There are no reliable figures; an estimated one and a half million to two million were gassed, shot, or hanged. Several thousand survived.

Crematorium. Ravensbrück KZ;
Fürstenberg, Germany

    *The first camp for women and
children only, Ravensbrück was also the
training center for women guards. There were
eventually 300 camps holding only women
and children, who were subjected to the same
treatment, labor, living conditions, punishment, torture, and death as men.*

Ruins of crematorium furnace. Sachsenhausen KZ; Sachsenhausen, Germany

Clay urns. Natzweiler KZ; near Le Struthof, France

For a payment ranging from 39 to 100 Reichsmark the family of a dead concentration camp prisoner could request an urn of ashes. Witnesses say that the urns were filled indiscriminately.

Memorial of ashes and bones. Sobibor Memorial; Sobibor, Poland
In the sixteen months of the death camp's operation between 200,000 and 250,000 people were gassed on arrival in carbon monoxide chambers and their bodies burned. The facility was later destroyed by the SS.

Ash pit. Birkenau KZ; Oswiecim, Poland
*Ashes from the five crematorium buildings, each containing several
ovens, were dumped here.*

Bones encased in crematorium. Majdanek KZ; near Lublin, Poland

Crematorium furnace. Dachau κz; Dachau, Germany
*All prisoners who died or were killed in the camps before the 1945
liberation were burned or buried in pits and have no marked graves.*

Corner of graveyard. Natzweiler KZ; near Le Struthof, France
*Marked graves at concentration camp sites are of prisoners who were
found dead by the Allies in 1945 or who died shortly afterwards.*

Marker of a mass grave. Chelmno extermination camp site;
Dabie, Poland

    *The first systematic gassing of Jews, in specially designed vans, began
here on December 8, 1941. In thirty-two months between 150,000 and
320,000 Jews, Gypsies, and the children of Lidice were killed here. Then the
Nazis destroyed the facility, now a memorial.*

Mass grave. Bergen Belsen KZ; Bergen, Germany

When British troops liberated the camp in 1945 they found 13,000 unburied corpses whom they buried in mass graves. Anne Frank and her sister Margot perished here a short time before the liberation.

Trees. Belzec extermination camp site; Belzec, Poland

Only three people are known to have escaped from this killing center in eastern Poland. During its ten-month operation in 1942 between 550,000 and 580,000 Jews, Poles who had tried to help them, and 2,000 Gypsies were gassed on arrival. Eventually the Nazis had the area plowed over and trees planted.

Barbed wire. Westerbork KZ; Westerbork, Netherlands

Barbed wire. Birkenau kz;
Oswiecim, Poland

Barbed wire and guard lights. Mauthausen KZ; Mauthausen, Austria

Barbed wire. Dachau KZ; Dachau, Germany

Barbed wire. Majdanek κz; near Lublin, Poland

Afterword

In times past the word *Dachau* referred to the picturesque old town a short train ride from Munich, the nearby moors long a favorite motif of landscape painters. Beginning in early 1933, when I was a teenager, shortly after the Nazis were elected to power in Germany and until the end of the war in 1945, Dachau came to mean the concentration camp that they had built on what were potato fields at the edge of town. Its official name was "Labor and Re-education Facility," but soon there were whispers, then rumors, and finally eyewitness reports that it was a place of brutality, of random violence and systematic destruction.

Dachau was destined to be the first of many such places, part of a precisely planned and organized system of concentration camps with clearly defined purposes—to eliminate all political opposition to the Nazi regime by means of terror, to use all able-bodied prisoners as forced labor for German industry until they were exhausted from starvation and overwork at which point they would be killed, and, finally, to destroy the spirit and the body of any man, woman, and child decreed undeserving of life according to the racial laws of the self-proclaimed "Master Race," among them homosexuals, Gypsies, members of charismatic Christian sects, and those handicapped in body or mind. And, of course, all Jews.

I had an early encounter with Dachau whose memory has never left me. I had a small accident in a fall from my bicycle and as I entered the waiting room of the nearby clinic two men were already there, one standing, the other sitting at the edge of the bench. The one standing wore the black uniform and boots and death head insignia of the SS, the other wore the gray-blue striped pajamas and wooden clogs of a Dachau inmate. His head was shaved, his face was gaunt and showed bruises. Neither spoke. I don't know why they were there. The SS guard looked out to the spring garden, the prisoner looked either onto the floor or, occasionally, also out of the room. They did not look at each other. Once the SS guard looked at me, without interest. In his eyes I saw the calm that comes from the possession of total physical power. My eyes and those of the prisoner did not meet, but I saw in them an emptiness that I had not ever seen before and in his face no expression of any kind. What I saw was the absence of expectation or hope—an expression of nothingness. I was soon called and my knee bandaged and on my way out the two men were no longer in the room. I saw neither of them again; I would recognize the prisoner to this day.

I had heard the phrase "blood running cold as ice"; now I knew what it meant. In that encounter I felt real fear and real terror for the first time in my life. I understood not only in my brain but in my guts what the Nazis were making of the Germany that was my home and that I loved—"an icy hell," as one Dachau survivor wrote. For a few minutes, even in that clean and antiseptic setting, I got a whiff of what it must be like to be a prisoner of the SS and I realized only later that I had seen the two faces of Nazi Germany—both the faces of death—that of the killer and that of the victim. The Nazis were turning a traditional and often overwrought German romanticism that had produced great literature and art into a worship of death that let loose on their enemies and ultimately on their own a systematic and barbaric orgy of killing. Death became the main instrument of the "Thousand-Year Reich" and the burden of its legacy to this day.

In the more than fifty years since then that I have lived in the United States I have never found an explanation for why my father was not put in a concentration camp. Like many others who were taken away, he was a middle-class Jew, successful in his work, a lifelong if passive Social Democrat, known and respected in the community. Perhaps he was spared because he had served and had been decorated for his years in the trenches of France as a soldier of the German army in World War I; in the beginning, at least, the Nazis seemed to have respect for patriotism, even for that of Jews. But if my mother had not had generous relatives in America who enabled the whole family—parents, two boys, and a little girl—to leave Germany in the summer of 1938, none of us would have escaped the camps much longer. Those of our relatives and many friends who could not leave—or would not leave—did not escape the camps and few survived.

I was sixteen when we left Germany. It was a wrench to lose what I had believed was my country and my language, it was difficult to begin growing new roots in a new home—at least it seemed so at the time. But soon, as bits and pieces of news drifted over from Europe, we came to understand that we had been spared a fate that was unbelievable even in the light of what we had experienced between 1933 and 1938: a legally elected German government was making of the country that had produced great philosophers and artists an instrument of systematic terror, brutality, slave labor, torture, and killing that consumed, like a wildfire, millions of innocent people, Jews and many others, in a frenzy of destruction. Eventually there were over a thousand camps and subcamps, a vast and dismal landscape of barbed wire across Germany and conquered Europe.

Not only we and other refugees from the Nazis, but the rest of the world, too, came to know of these deeds long before the end of the war, and soon everyone also knew that the majority of Germans had done little to protest, and very little to defeat the increasingly violent seduction of their own country and the rape of many other countries in Europe. In Germany the phrase "we did not know what they did" is still current and my response still is "how strange that you did not know—*we* knew what they were doing." The phrase "we did not want to know what they did" is not often heard.

I volunteered for military service on the morning after Pearl Harbor and had to wait a year to be accepted since I was still an "enemy alien" and classified as a "premature antifascist." But finally I was inducted and spent three years in the U.S. Army, most of them in Europe, the usual "Grand Tour"—England, France, Belgium, Germany—and when the war was over and we had won, I believed that I had paid off a debt of gratitude to the United States, the country that had taken us in and thus had saved our lives.

Not long after V-E Day, while I was stationed in Augsburg, I drove to the concentration camp in Dachau. By then the many dead that had been found piled up on the ground by the liberating Allied troops had been buried and most of the barracks had been emptied and leveled to stop the further spread of diseases. As a part of the makeshift display for visitors in one of the remaining barracks a prisoner's uniform had been put near the door, with a sign hung from the neck that said "ICH BIN WIEDER DA," "I AM BACK," recalling prisoners who had tried to escape and been recaptured, made to stand with that sign hung on them on the parade ground, then been slowly and systematically beaten to death in the presence of the entire prisoner population that had been assembled for the purpose.

I remember feeling that the sign also referred to me, that I was once again where I had been born, returned from my safe new home, confronted with what had happened to people like me. I knew then that the terror I had felt when I saw the prisoner and the SS guard in the clinic had been an accurate omen of a fate that could have befallen me as well, and that I did not know why it had passed me over. For a long time afterwards I believed that by having served in the liberation of Europe I had also helped to stop any further suffering and slaughter in the camps and that whatever debt I owed to those who had been tortured and killed there had been paid.

But, apparently, some debts are not easily settled. Over the years and increasingly in the recent past I came to feel a summons to return to the remains of the camps. It did not come suddenly and it was never precise, rather it consisted of subtle, sometimes ambiguous, and always unexpected "messages" such as what happened a few years ago when my son and I were in Munich at the same time on separate work, a rare occurrence. We decided that afterwards we would take a short holiday together, "but first," he said, "show me the camp at Dachau," and that is where we began the journey. Like me, he prefers solitude to tour guides, hence there was little talking or explaining and as we left he took my arm and said, "I was thinking that I might have lost you right here."

Finally I came to the realization that now, toward the end of my working life as a photographer and close to the fiftieth anniversary of the liberation of the last camps, the person and the photographer had to come together as never before to make images in what remains of the camps and of what there is still to be seen in them. I had photographed in some camps occasionally and casually during earlier trips to Europe, but now it was to be a journey undertaken for this purpose alone. I had no illusions; there would be nothing of fact that I could add to the existing voluminous documentation of the camps, and I knew also that my being in the camps or photographing in them would bring no one back from the dead or ease the suffering of any survivor. I simply felt obliged to stand in as many of the camps as I could reach, to fulfill a duty that I could not define and to pay a belated tribute with the tools of my profession.

In the middle of last winter I journeyed to the camp sites and to the other places which are shown in this book. The weather was fitting—nearly always overcast and wet; often there was snow on the ground and sometimes heavy fog in the air. The days were short and most of the time it was half dark even at noon. In the great stillness I heard little except the barking of dogs, the crunch of my shoes on the ground, sometimes the throb of my pulse. Even when my wife was along it was a voyage of silence; words are of no avail there. Visitors, if any, were few—it was the season of holidays and school vacations.

I was surprised at the intensity with which even after so many years the camps seemed still inhabited by the echoes of the dark and bitter past. Every day that

I spent walking through former camps I wanted nothing more than to leave again as quickly as possible, and every day I was grateful that instead of just being there I had a camera, a machine without feelings of its own, with which to attempt to express what I felt. I am convinced that I would not have survived in any of the camps.

The journey took a little over eight weeks. In Poland, where we had never been before, we had a driver/guide/interpreter; we traveled to Theresienstadt by night train from Germany to Prague and drove the rest of the way; elsewhere I rented cars as I needed them. There were occasional days of housekeeping and rest, even of celebration. We spent New Year's Eve in Hamburg in the quiet lounge of our small hotel in the company of two other couples presumably also far away from home and watched over by a gentle bartender with a generous supply of the traditional crullers and Sekt, the German champagne. If there was any music it was so soft that it did not disturb and there was little talk; each person was respectful of the others' private thoughts. Mine were predictable—I had spent Christmas Day alone in a thick and cold fog in the Buchenwald concentration camp before driving to the vicinity of Bergen Belsen in the early dusk; at this moment I was in a festive place in the comfort of beloved company; in a day's time we were leaving for the death camps of the SS in Poland, not only designed to do away with the Jews and Gypsies and homosexuals of Europe, but designed also, later on, to get rid of the millions of Soviet prisoners of war whom the German army expected to capture, and, later still, to empty the fertile Polish and Ukrainian plains of their inhabitants so that German immigrant settlers would have "Lebensraum" once Germany had won the war. I felt warm and cold at the same time, I was at my ease and on edge at the same time, it was a breather between the unjoyous memories of weeks past and the anticipation of weeks to come.

When we returned a month later I thought that I had been to the bottom of the Nazis' inhumanities but I had not; it was at an obscure memorial in Hamburg not long after we came back from Poland where the full extent and enormity of the Nazis' deadly rage flooded over us. Ruth Bains Hartmann, my wife, wrote about it in her journal:

Each time one thinks to have looked into the farthest depths of human cruelty, the abyss awaits. After all the horrible things I had seen, all the places of human suffering—at the hand of man—I had witnessed, how could I imagine anything worse?

There is a small rose garden in an industrial area of Hamburg, not far from one of the city's many canals. Irregularly shaped, the garden's wooden fencing separates it on one side from a busy highway, on the other from the play-yard of a nursery school where on a wintry morning brightly dressed toddlers splashed happily in frigid puddles until a teacher shepherded them towards less dangerous play.

On the far side of the playground is the Bullenhuser Damm School, in the Nazi time a sub-camp of Neuengamme, the concentration camp near Hamburg, now renamed as the Janusz Korczak School, for the head of the Warsaw orphanage who died with his children in the Treblinka gas chamber.

A few days before the end of the war twenty Jewish children were taken by the SS to the Bullenhuser Damm School together with two French doctors and two Dutch men, their caretakers, all prisoners. In November 1944 these children, ten boys and ten girls (the Nazis were ever methodical) aged from five to twelve years, had been brought from Auschwitz to Neuengamme where they were subjected to medical experiments by the SS doctor Kurt Heissmeyer. The children were injected with TB bacillus, making them very ill, then their lymph glands were removed for analysis.

On the night of April 20, 1945, with British troops not far from Hamburg, the SS took these children, together with the four men, to the furnace room in the cellar of the school where they were hanged. Hanged. The youngest ones were five years old.

There were millions of victims at Auschwitz; one struggles to imagine even one million. The reality of those millions of tortured lives and horrible murders can hardly be grasped. In the atrocity of the hanging of twenty young children one's imagination is vivid. Some of these children were perhaps as young as three when they were taken from their homes in Italy, France, Poland, Holland, Yugoslavia, transported hundreds of miles in filthy railroad cars, separated from their families, transported again, tortured methodically and lengthily and then destroyed, hanged in a cellar. This one can imagine; they can stand for the millions:

> *Marek James, six years old, from Radom in Poland*
> *H. Wassermann, an eight-year-old girl from Poland*
> *Roman Witonski, six years old, and his five-year-old sister Eleonora,*
>   *from Radom in Poland*
> *R. Zeller, a twelve-year-old boy from Poland*
> *Eduard Hornemann, twelve years old, and his brother Alexander, nine years old,*
>   *from Eindhoven in Holland*
> *Riwka Herszberg, a seven-year-old girl from Zdunska Wola in Poland*
> *Georges André Kohn, twelve years old, from Paris*
> *Jacqueline Morgenstern, twelve years old, from Paris*
> *Ruchla Zylberberg, an eight-year-old girl*
> *Edouard Reichenbaum, ten years old*
> *Mania Altman, five years old, from Radom in Poland*
> *Sergio de Simone, seven years old, from Naples*
> *Marek Steinbaum, ten years old*
> *W. Junglieb, a twelve-year-old boy*
> *S. Goldinger, an eleven-year-old girl*
> *Lelka Birnbaum, a twelve-year-old girl*
> *Lola Kugerman, twelve years old*
> *B. Mekler, an eleven-year-old girl*

Before the abominations of Treblinka, of Sobibor and Belzec, of Dachau, Birkenau, Chelmno and all the rest, one can feel anger, sorrow, pity, rage, nausea, anxiety for the human race, but in the rose garden behind the Bullenhuser Damm School one can only weep.

The weak winter sunshine picked out the bright green of the early shoots of spring flowers among the sleeping rosebushes. Then a black cloud came over and freezing rain poured down over the garden as I stood there reading the names on the memorial plaques that line the fence.

As the murders of these children can stand for the murders of millions, so can the inscription in their memorial garden speak for all the places of terror and death:

WHEN YOU STAND HERE, BE SILENT;

WHEN YOU LEAVE HERE, BE NOT SILENT.

The passage of time is unstoppable. The number of survivors diminishes every day and soon there will be no one—neither victim nor perpetrator—who was there. Soon the entire physical fabric—buildings and authentic objects—will have disintegrated and will have had to be completely replaced by reconstructions, as for instance the seemingly endless miles of rusting barbed wire are already having to be replaced every few years. Hence, the functions of the camp sites will change from being mainly places of memory and reminder to becoming mainly museums and educational sites, their physical area to be reduced in many places. Photographs such as these may not be possible much longer.

There is good reason to believe that the function of the existing camp sites will change significantly and perhaps soon. At present their main purpose is to document and to describe what happened there and how. That has been difficult enough because of the Nazis' often successful efforts to obliterate all evidence ahead of the liberating armies. It is a sanitized documentation at best—what is left of the camps today is clean, whereas they were filthy when they were in use; now they are quiet, whereas they were filled with noises then—the screams of guards, the snarls of dogs, the sounds of shuffling feet, snoring, coughing, moaning. Today the camps are empty and no trace is left of the endemic overcrowding, lack of water, of heat, of food, and of any of the basic decencies of life that led soon to outbreaks of diseases and epidemics. Many survivors have said that having no privacy of any kind was among the most difficult parts of camp life to bear.

On this journey I realized once more that, even after the many years since the liberation of the concentration camps, the Nazi past has not been put to rest. In Germany it is nearly palpable, the uninvited and often unexpected guest in many phases of public and personal life. The memory of what some Germans did and most Germans chose not to notice remains an irritant, like an open wound that keeps hurting and does not heal. In the casual and sometimes serious conversations that happen during traveling, in which I was usually taken for a German and in which my purpose for being there usually remained unsaid, the past would often and sometimes quickly become the main subject, sometimes with an intensity that verged on compulsion, like an addiction that one fights against but in the end yields to— ever present, allowing no final conclusion, no resolution. I was not surprised that I recognized no consensus of what the Germans think should happen about the Nazi past; I found instead a clear division:

Many, perhaps most, Germans believe that there is a continuing obligation to remember what happened in the camps and the reasons why it happened and was allowed to happen, and who believe also that Germany has a continuing responsibility to try to prevent it from happening again.

But there are some Germans who think otherwise. The remains of the charred "Jews' barracks" at the Sachsenhausen camp memorial site are one of many examples in Germany today in which a very different view of the past and a very different message for the future are unmistakably voiced. Expressed in the defacement and destruction of cemeteries and synagogues, in fires set to destroy the stores and homes of foreigners and intended to burn their inhabitants to death, it is a message that appears more than occasionally these days not only in such deeds but in the statements of some radical parties and in the speeches of some radical politicians. The words may vary but the meaning is always the same: you Jews and all you immigrants from Eastern Europe or wherever else you have come from, you are not Germans, you are not welcome here. Go away and when you leave take with you the memory of what you say was done to you by Germans. We don't believe most of it, but if anyone did it to you it was our grandparents, not we. We are tired of the mark of Cain that you have put on our foreheads, we have carried the burden of guilt long enough. Go away.

It is hard to foresee which of these messages—responsibility or denial—will prevail in Germany; the circumstances and elements that contribute to such decisions change constantly. It is not a German problem alone. Brutality and the destruction of "undesirables" for political ends have happened elsewhere since 1945 and are still happening—the earth is strewn with the evidence. The idea that was brought to a high state of the art of killing by the Nazis is alive and well and it has been improved upon since 1945.

Standing in the Auschwitz gas chamber I was confronted with the realities of deliberate and cold-blooded killing as never before, not even during the war. It was an experience that I will not be able to forget, it was a reminder of what human beings were capable of doing to other human beings when passion and rage took the place of reason and basic decency. I realized again how easy it is in these days of high technology for the relatively few without conscience to take away the freedoms and spirit and the lives of the many who are at their mercy. I came to understand that I was not safe—that no one anywhere is safe—from these dangers because the line that divides victors from victims—and good from evil—is thin and elastic.

If I have learned any lesson from having been in the remains of the camps it is that thinking or living for oneself alone has become an unaffordable luxury. Except perhaps in dreams, life no longer takes place on a solitary plane, it is now irrevocably complex, and we, whoever we are, have become intertwined one with the other whether we like it or not. Acting on that belief may be a more effective tribute to the memory of the dead than mourning alone or vowing that it shall not happen again, and it may also be the most promising way of doing away with the concentration camps. I am not an optimist, but I believe that if we decide that we must link our lives inextricably—that "me" and "them" must be replaced by "us"—we may manage to make a life in which gas chambers will not be used again anywhere and a future in which children, including my granddaughters, will not know what they are.

Erich Hartmann
New York, September 1994

Rose garden memorial at the Janusz Korczak School.
Bullenhuser Damm; Hamburg, Germany

Plaque to a murdered child.
Bullenhuser Damm; Hamburg, Germany

"Judenbaracken"—the Jews' barracks. Sachsenhausen KZ; Sachsenhausen, Germany

The two barracks numbered 38 and 39, where Jews were kept, were set on fire in September 1992. The police apprehended young right-wing radicals from Berlin and they were put on trial, then acquitted "for lack of sufficient evidence." A tent was erected over the ruins to prevent further deterioration. Discussions have been in progress, so far without results, between German authorities and interested organizations to decide whether to rebuild the barracks to their former condition as a museum or to leave them in their present state as a memorial.

Gas chamber (never used). Dachau KZ; Dachau, Germany

About the photographs

Of the many photographic projects that I have done, this one made the severest demands on finding a balance between motivation and technique. All photographs result from a fusing of the personal and professional, and before I went to the camps I realized that I would have to work there with a particular state of mind: I wanted as much as possible to concentrate on the non-photographic reasons for being there, to do homage, to accomplish a *Liebesdienst;* I did not want to make descriptive photographs of the concentration camps, but to express what landscape, architecture, and objects would say to me about the past, their meaning in the present, and the implications for the future.

Hence the strenuous parts of this project had to do neither with photographing nor with the discomforts of winter. I tried to listen with my eyes and, stimulated by what I saw, I photographed quickly and impulsively, accepting places and objects and such variables as the weather and time of day as I found them, instead of arranging things, bringing additional lighting, or returning when I thought the existing light was more appropriate, as I have done on many other occasions.

As a result I worked in simple ways. My equipment was no more elaborate than what any visitor might have used—35-mm single reflex cameras and lenses. Nearly always I used 400 ASA film, 1600 ASA when I had to. In the car I had some backup items—an extra camera body, extra film, a tripod, a strobe. I used the tripod once and the strobe not at all. The limited opening times of the camp museums in winter made for short days, although some camp sites themselves were open longer. I needed no special permissions and received no privileges except once when, through the kindness of a museum director, I was able to photograph on a rest day, thus saving some time. Since I was a long way from home I had the exposed films developed at a professional lab in Hamburg whenever I returned from one of the several legs of which the journey consisted. I would examine each new batch of processed films for technical details such as sharpness and negative quality; I did not look seriously at any for their photographic contents until I was finished and back in New York.

The project consumed a total of 126 rolls of film, from which I made a preliminary selection of about 300 frames; of those I had reference prints made on 8 x 10-inch RC (resin-coated) paper. The 74 images in this book were printed for reproduction on RC paper once again, somewhat contrary to the methods of many other photographers. I believe that if the paper contrast is chosen with care, RC paper yields a richness of tonal range equal to that from prints made on a fiber base.

Debts of gratitude

Among the many people who helped in the making of this book I owe special thanks to:

Howard Squadron. His friendship and counsel in this as in many other matters have been more than generous.

Anna Elisabeth Rosmus, *The Nasty Girl*. Her conscience and single-minded pursuit of facts about the Third Reich have been an inspiration since we first met many years ago.

Holger Thoss and Philippe Cheng. Individually and together they sacrificed large amounts of time and paper in the making of the enlargements of the photographs.

Gunter Thoss, Holger's father. His remarkable hospitality warmed our bodies and gave comfort to our spirits at a cold time, his open-hearted help to us in Poland made my work there effective and less difficult than it most assuredly would otherwise have been.

Lidia Sykulak, our guide and driver in Poland. She interpreted for us with care and patience in places and of things that were unfamiliar and painful to her, she introduced us to the mysteries of Polish cuisine, she was uncomplaining of my insistent schedule, and she drove us with more skill and confidence than anyone with whom I have ever been in a car.

Margot Klingsporn, Magnum's agent in Hamburg. She gave her love to this project and to us, her office became my office during the nearly three months of being in and out of Hamburg; she provided hotels, money, film, processing, telephone, fax, and everything else I needed. Her generosity to us has been enormous and so is my gratitude to her.

Milton Glaser. His encouragement and help on behalf of this book made possible the first steps of its journey.

Peter Mayer and Robert Dreeson. I thank them for their interest and kindness to me and for their understanding.

Inge Morath, my dear Magnum colleague. She gave me much needed photographic encouragement and very much appreciated personal help.

Dr. Peter Fischer, the representative in the former East Berlin of the Central Council of Jews in Germany. It was through him that I came to understand the feelings of many Jews now living in Germany about the bitter years from 1933 to 1945 and since.

Frances Collin, for her act of faith and for her help along the many steps to the completion of this book.

I am most of all indebted to:

Nathan Garland. He has been devoted to this work from the start and has contributed much more to it than the graphic design alone. The many hours of work with him have deepened my respect for his skills and my admiration for his heart.

Jim Mairs. In making this book with him I have come to admire his understanding of photographs and photographers, his amazing ability to take an obstacle and turn it into an advantage, and his photographer's devotion to another photographer's work. This book bears many marks of his imagination and courage. I cannot thank him enough.

Designed by Nathan Garland,
New Haven, Connecticut

Composed in a modern version
of Bembo by Ken Scaglia

Printed in duotone and bound
by Arnaldo Mondadori Editore,
Verona, Italy

Barbed wire. Buchenwald KZ;
near Weimar, Germany (back endpapers)